THE *Sketchbook* ADVENTURES of

PETER POPLASKI

DENIS KITCHEN PUBLISHING CO., LLC
AMHERST, MASSACHUSETTS

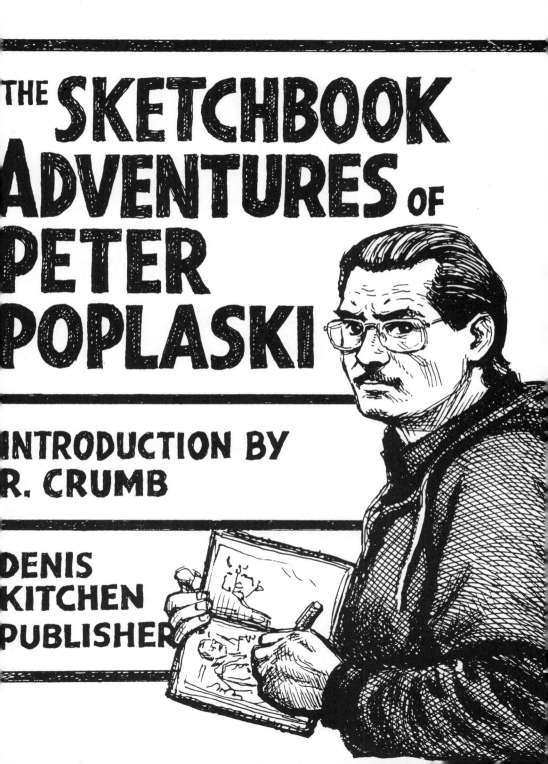

THE SKETCHBOOK ADVENTURES OF PETER POPLASKI

INTRODUCTION BY R. CRUMB

DENIS
KITCHEN
PUBLISHER

PUBLISHER - DENIS KITCHEN
DESIGN AND PRODUCTION - PETER POPLASKI AND JOHN LIND

THE SKETCHBOOK ADVENTURES OF PETER POPLASKI
Copyright © 2005 by Peter Poplaski.
Introduction copyright © 2005 by R.Crumb.

Denis Kitchen Publishing Co., LLC
P.O. Box 2250, Amherst, MA 01004-2250
www.deniskitchenpublishing.com

For original art by Peter Poplaski, Will Eisner, Harvey Kurtzman and other
fine artists, go to the Steve Krupp Gallery at www.deniskitchen.com

First printing: April 2005

5 4 3 2 1

ISBN No. 0-9710080-4-3

Printed in China

THIS BOOK IS DEDICATED TO
ALINE KOMINSKY-CRUMB
WHOSE GENEROSITY GOES
BEYOND THE DEFINITION
OF THE WORD.

INTRODUCTION
by R. Crumb

I'VE KNOWN PETE POPLASKI FOR A LONG TIME — SINCE THE MID-1970S. WHEN I FIRST MET HIM HE WAS WORKING FOR DENIS KITCHEN'S LITTLE COMIC BOOK COMPANY, "KRUPP COMIC WORKS", IN PRINCETON, WISCONSIN. HE WAS NEVER OFFICIALLY ON THE PAY-ROLL. DENIS WOULD GIVE HIM CASH AS HE NEEDED IT— A VERY INFORMAL ARRANGEMENT. HE STRUCK ME RIGHT AWAY AS A VIVID, HIGHLY INDIVIDUAL CHARACTER, WITH A BOY-ISH ENTHUSIASM AND ENERGY THAT WAS INFECTIOUS. HE WAS, ALREADY IN HIS MID-TWENTIES, AN ACCOMPLISHED ARTIST, PRODUCING DRAWINGS AND PAINTINGS OF EXCEPTIONAL QUALITY. EVEN WAY BACK THEN I URGED KITCHEN TO PUBLISH SOME OF HIS SKETCHBOOK MATERIAL (HE DIDN'T). I COULD SEE IMMEDIATELY THAT HE WAS BURNING WITH FERVENT IDEALISM AND DEDICATION TO HIS ART, TO THE LIFE OF THE ARTIST, TO THE HISTORY OF ART (AS OF THIS WRITING HE HAS VISITED MORE ART MUS-EUMS THAN ANY OTHER HUMAN BEING ON THE PLANET, I FEEL CERTAIN), TO COMICS, MOV-IES, TELEVISION. HE HAD THEN, AND STILL HAS, AMONG HIS HEROES DOUGLAS FAIR-BANKS AND BUSTER KEATON, AND EMULATED THEIR WAY OF LEAPING ABOUT AND BLITHE-LY TAKING PRATFALLS. HE HAD A GREAT FONDNESS FOR THE COMIC BOOK SUPER HER-OES, AND SINCERELY BELIEVED IN THE OLD HEROIC IDEALS WHICH THEY STOOD FOR. I WOULD SAY HE HASN'T CHANGED MUCH OVER THE DECADES I'VE KNOWN HIM, EXCEPT THAT HIS KNOWLEDGE IN HIS VARIOUS FIELDS OF INTEREST IS MORE REFINED, MORE EXTENSIVE. THE BOYISH ENTHUSIASM HAS SURVIVED INTACT; THE IDEALISM AND DEDICATION TO ART IS STILL THE CENT-RAL THEME OF HIS LIFE. HE IS STILL UNMARRIED AT AGE FIFTY, OWNS NO REAL ESTATE, LIVES QUITE SPONTANEOUSLY. TO HIS FAMILY HE HAS BEEN RATHER A DISAPPOINTMENT. THEY WOULD VERY MUCH LIKE TO SEE HIM IN A SECURE, COMFORTABLE POSITION IN THE WORLD, WITH A NICE WIFE AND SOME NICE KIDS. PETE MAY SUFFER FROM SOME ANXIETY OVER THESE EXPECTATIONS OF HIS PARENTS AND RELATIVES, BUT MY OBSERVATION HAS BEEN THAT HE WILL ALWAYS JUMP FREE OF ANY "ADULT"-TYPE COMMITMENT THAT PRESENTS ITSELF, WHETHER IT BE A STEADY JOB OR A WOMAN WHO WOULD LIKE TO SET UP HOUSEKEEPING WITH HIM. "I'M A COWBOY", SAYS PETE. HE'D JUST AS SOON EAT OUT OF A CAN AND GO TO BED IN HIS FUNKY OLD SLEEPING BAG. I'VE NEVER KNOWN HIM TO OFFICIALLY OWN A CAR OR HAVE A FUNCTIONING TELEPHONE. MONEY BURNS A HOLE IN HIS POCKET. HIS FAMILY, THE POPLASKIS IN GREEN BAY, ARE SOLID MIDWEST-ERNERS, AND THEY DON'T SEE THE POINT. "PETE, WHAT ARE YOU DOING WITH YOUR LIFE," THEY ASK DURING HIS VISITS HOME. HE HAS NO READY ANSWER FOR THEM. HOW DOES ONE EXPLAIN SUCH A WAY OF LIFE? HE FEELS BAD ABOUT IT— IT HAUNTS HIM BECAUSE HE STILL HAS STRONG TIES TO THEM AND KNOWS THAT THEY'LL NEVER UNDERSTAND THE LIFE HE'S CHOSEN. SURE, THEY ADMIRE HIS ARTISTIC SKILLS, BUT WHEN IS HE GOING TO SETTLE DOWN? WHERE'S THAT WIFE HE SHOULD'VE HAD BY NOW? WHERE ARE THOSE GRANDCHILDREN THEY'VE BEEN WAITING AND HOPING TO SEE? WHERE'S THE NICE HOUSE, THE CAR, THE RECREATIONAL VEHICLE??

THERE'S NO WAY TO EXPLAIN TO THESE GOOD PEOPLE WHAT IT TAKES TO BE A SINCERE, DEDICATED ARTIST IN THIS WORLD. A LOT OF THINGS HAVE TO GO BY THE WAYSIDE. THE IDEAL IS TO CONCENTRATE ON THE WORK. THE MORE FOCUSED ENERGY YOU CAN PUT INTO THE ART, THE BETTER THE ART WILL BE. ENERGY IS A FINITE THING AND IF IT'S NOT USED WISELY WE GET NOWHERE. IT'S A BATTLE EVERY DAY. YOU GOTTA BE A WARRIOR, AS PETE SAYS. BETTER THAT PETE HAS STEERED CLEAR OF ALL THOSE "NORMAL" RESPONSIBILITIES THAN IF HE HAD TAKEN THEM ON AND THEN BEHAVED IRRESPONSIBLY. HE HAS MADE THE CHOICE FOR ART AND HAD THE CLARITY OF PURPOSE TO STICK TO IT. THAT IS UNUSUAL AND COMMENDABLE.

PETE FIRST ARRIVED IN THIS VILLAGE HERE IN FRANCE ABOUT TEN YEARS AGO, ABOUT A YEAR AFTER I MOVED HERE WITH MY WIFE AND DAUGHTER. HE CAME WITH DENIS KIT-CHEN TO ATTEND THE ANNUAL COMICS FESTIVAL IN THE CITY OF ANGOULÊME, AND AFTER-WARD THEY CAME DOWN HERE TO VISIT ME. HE LIKED IT HERE, LIKED THE WAY EVERY-THING LOOKED, THE OLD STONE HOUSES, THE DRAMATIC, ROCKY TERRAIN, "LIKE A MOVIE SET", HE EXCLAIMED. HE CAME BACK AND STAYED LONGER EACH TIME. THE LOOSE, CASUAL, "LAISSEZ FAIRE" ATMOSPHERE SUITED HIM. HE FOUND THAT HE COULD LIVE HERE ON AL-MOST NOTHING. HE WOULD DO SOME COMMERCIAL WORK FOR AMERICAN COMIC PUBLISHERS OCCASIONALLY, OR SELL AN OIL PAINTING NOW AND THEN, AND MAKE ENOUGH TO GET BY. HE SPENT THE LARGER PART OF HIS MEAGER EARNINGS COLLECTING OLD ZORRO MOVIE POSTERS. ALINE AND I BOUGHT SOME OF HIS PAINTINGS, AND ALINE PITCHED THEM TO HER PROSPER-OUS GERMAN FRIENDS, AND THEY NOW OWN TWO OR THREE POPLASKIS. WE CONSIDERED THEM BARGAINS. WE WERE GETTING IN ON THE GROUND FLOOR, US AND A FEW OTHERS, BEFORE THE REST OF THE WORLD CAUGHT ON. YES, WE ARE SUPREMELY CONFIDENT OF OUR DIS-CERNING TASTE IN ALL AESTHETIC MATTERS. PETE HAS PRODUCED MANY GORGEOUS TOWN-AND LANDSCAPES, STILL-LIFES AND PORTRAITS IN OIL, CHARCOAL, WATER COLOR, AND

PEN-AND-INK SINCE HE'S BEEN LIVING HERE. HIS WORK HABITS ARE IDIOSYNCRATIC TO SAY THE LEAST, BUT WHEN YOU SEE THE RESULTS, THE STRIKING PICTURES HE TURNS OUT, THERE'S NOTHING MORE TO SAY ABOUT IT. THAT'S THE MYSTERIOUS MIRACLE OF THE HUMAN CREATIVE PROCESS.

PETE IS ONE OF THESE ARTISTS WHO ALWAYS TOTES A SKETCHBOOK. HE'S BEEN PILING UP SKETCHBOOKS FOR DECADES. THESE BOOKS ARE A VISUAL DIARY OF HIS LIFE, SAME AS MINE ARE FOR ME. IF YOU ARE THE TYPE OF PERSON WHO GETS ENJOY-MENT FROM LOOKING AT FINE DRAWING, THEN YOU ARE IN FOR HOURS OF PLEASURE WITH THIS BOOK, FOR HEREIN ARE NEARLY 200 PAGES DENSELY PACKED WITH DRAWINGS OF HUMAN FACES AND FIGURES, BUILDINGS, ROCKS AND TREES, ALL RENDERED IN A MANNER BOTH PLEASING TO THE EYE AND PENETRATING OF THE SUBJECT. EVERYTHING IS DRAWN WITH CHARACTER, ESSENSE AND VITALITY. ALL THE FACES ARE OF REAL, LIVE HUMAN BEINGS, INDIVIDUAL AND UNIQUE. THE LINES TELL A STORY, A NARRATIVE TAKEN DIRECT-LY FROM THE REAL WORLD. THE ARTIST IS FIRMLY CONVINCED THAT DRAWING FROM LIFE PRODUCES THE STRONGEST, MOST AUTHENTIC ART. EVERY SINGLE DRAWING IN THIS BOOK WAS MADE FROM LIFE. THE PEOPLE WERE DRAWN IN CAFÉS, RESTAURANTS, WAIT-ING ROOMS OF TRAIN STATIONS, BUS DEPOTS, AIRPORTS — ANY PUBLIC PLACE WHERE HUM-ANS ARE FOUND SITTING AROUND. THE ARTIST HAS TO WORK FAST AND TRY NOT TO BE TOO OBVIOUS. IT'S BEST IF THE SUBJECTS ARE UNAWARE THAT THEY'RE BEING "CAPTURED." I HAVE BEEN WITH PETE IN PLACES SUCH AS THESE AND WATCHED HIM SURREPTITIOUSLY DRAW-ING PEOPLE. HE'S GOOD AT NOT BEING NOTICED. HIS SKETCHBOOK IS SMALL, AND HE DOESN'T LOOK LIKE AN ARTIST. NOT AT ALL. HE LOOKS LIKE THE MAN WHO READS METERS FOR THE UTILITY COMPANY. LATER, AT HIS LEISURE, HE WILL OFTEN TIGHTEN UP AND REFINE THESE CANDID PORTRAITS, GIVE THEM MORE SOLIDITY. THERE'S A DRAWING OF ME IN HERE, ONE OF THE HUNDREDS OF HEADS. HE DID IT SITTING NEXT TO ME IN THE BACK SEAT OF A MOVING CAR. THERE ARE SEVERAL OF ALINE, AND MANY OF OTHER PERSONAL FRIENDS MIXED IN WITH THE TOTAL STRANGERS. MOST OF THE OUTDOOR SCENES, OLD STONE BUILDINGS, RUINS, AND ROCKY LANDSCAPES ARE FROM THIS VILLAGE AND ITS SURROUNDINGS. THIS BOOK IS COMPILED OF DRAWINGS FROM SEVERAL SKETCHBOOKS FILLED UP SINCE THE ARTIST HAS BEEN LIVING HERE IN THE SOUTH OF FRANCE WITH PERIODIC SOJOURNS BACK IN THE U.S.A.

THE CUMULATIVE EFFECT, ON ME, OF LOOKING AT POPLASKI'S SKETCHBOOKS IS AN OPTIMISTIC FEELING, AN AFFIRMATION OF LIFE, OF PEOPLE. THIS IS GOOD FOR ME—A TON-IC FOR A CURMUDGEON SUCH AS MYSELF, WHO TENDS TOWARD A BLEAK, DESPAIRING OUTLOOK. ALL THE PEOPLE IN THIS BOOK APPEAR HEROIC, EACH IN THEIR OWN PERSONAL WAY, IN THEIR OWN STRUGGLE FOR SURVIVAL, BECAUSE PETE'S SPIRIT IS ESSENTIALLY POSITIVE, BUOYANT, RESILIANT, AND THIS SHINES THROUGH IN ALL HIS DRAWINGS AND PAINTINGS. IT IS THIS POSITIVE SPIRIT THAT GIVES HIS ARTISTIC SKILL ITS REAL REASON AND PURPOSE FOR BEING.

—— R. CRUMB
SAUVE, FRANCE
FEBRUARY, 2002

DRAWINGS FROM FIVE
SKETCHBOOKS FROM
1994 TO 2002 !

STUDY of
MICHELANGELO'S "VICTORY"
IN THE PALAZZO VECCHIO
MAY 3 1994
FIRENZE

⑨

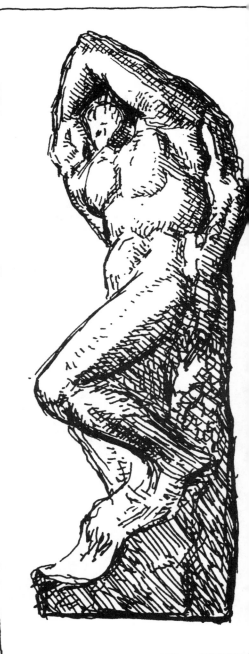

STUDIES AT THE GALLERIA DELL' ACCADEMIA, MAY 4, 19
"FINISHED-UNFINISHED"   "THE PRISONER"
MICHELANGELO

⑩

OLD MAN AT
"NATION"
METRO
STOP · PARIS

JUNE 17, 1994

aimez vos ennemis

SAT

"MAKE IT FOUR QUOTES AND BRING ME A GALLON!

YAH, SHOEER!

" ... TO LIVE CREATIVELY, I HAVE DISCOVERED, MEANS TO LIVE MORE AND MORE UNSELFISHLY, TO LIVE MORE AND MORE *INTO* THE WORLD, IDENTIFYING ONESELF WITH IT AND THUS INFLUENCING IT AT THE CORE, SO TO SPEAK. **ART**, LIKE RELIGION, IT NOW SEEMS TO ME, IS ONLY A PREPARATION, AN INITIATION INTO THE WAY OF LIFE. THE GOAL IS LIBERATION, FREEDOM, WHICH MEANS ASSUMING GREATER RESPONSIBILITY. TO CONTINUE WRITING BEYOND THE POINT OF SELF-REALIZATION SEEMS FUTILE AND ARRESTING. THE MASTERY OF ANY FORM OF EXPRESSION SHOULD LEAD INEVITABLY TO THE FINAL EXPRESSION — MASTERY OF LIFE. IN THIS REALM ONE IS ABSOLUTELY ALONE - FACE TO FACE WITH THE VERY ELEMENTS OF CREATION. IT IS AN EXPERIMENT WHOSE OUTCOME NOBODY CAN PREDICT. IF IT BE SUCCESSFUL THE WHOLE WORLD IS AFFECTED AND IN A WAY NEVER KNOWN BEFORE." — HENRY MILLER
"*THE COLOSSUS of MAROUSSI*"

12

— GROUCHO MARX

HARRY ROWOHLT
AT LA TOUR
DE MOLE
RESTAURANT
SAUVE
1994

"THE BASIC PROJECT OF ART IS ALWAYS TO MAKE THE WORLD WHOLE AND COMPREHENSIBLE, TO RESTORE IT TO US IN ALL ITS GLORY AND ITS OCCASIONAL NASTINESS, NOT THROUGH ARGUMENT BUT THROUGH FEELING, AND THEN TO CLOSE THE GAP BETWEEN YOU AND EVERYTHING THAT IS NOT YOU AND IN THIS WAY PASS FROM FEELING TO MEANING. IT'S NOT SOMETHING THAT COMMITTEES CAN DO. IT'S NOT A TASK ACHIEVED BY GROUPS OR BY MOVEMENTS. IT'S DONE BY INDIVIDUALS, EACH PERSON MEDIATING IN SOME WAY BETWEEN A SENSE OF HISTORY AND AN EXPERIENCE OF THE WORLD."
— ROBERT HUGHES
"SHOCK OF THE NEW" TV
SERIES - EPISODE 8, 1980.

"QUI CHERCHE LA VÉRITÉ DOIT ÊTRE PRÊT À L'INATTENDU, CAR ELLE EST DIFFICILE À TROUVER, ET QUAND ON LA RENCONTRE, DE CONCERTANTE."
— HERACLITE

"THE VITALITY OF ARTISTIC EXPRESSION IS ESSENTIALLY AUTO-BIOGRAPHICAL. THE CREATION OF A PICTURE, A POEM, A MUSICAL COMPOSITION, IS A RECORD OF THE ARTIST'S EMOTIONAL AND SPIRITUAL REACTION TO LIFE AND ITS TRADITIONS. THIS IS TRUE, WHETHER THE SENSES DEAL WITH BEAUTY IN THE ABSTRACT OR WITH THE TANGIBLE DRAMA AND POETRY OF EVERYDAY EXISTENCE. THERE IS ALSO THAT STIMULATING AND VALUABLE SPIRIT OF PROTEST WHICH IS INEVITABLY A FACTOR IN THE AGITATION TOWARD PERSONAL EXPRESSION —— THE PROTEST AGAINST UNSATISFYING EXISTING STANDARDS OR OF TRADITION."
— N.C. WYETH

13

MARIE CHRISTINE AT LE MICOCOULIER RESTAURANT — OCTOBER 14, 1994

" MY ART IS REPRESENTATIONAL BY CHOICE. IN MY OPINION, IF THE ART OF PAINTING IS TO SURVIVE, IT MUST DESCRIBE AND EXPRESS PEOPLE, THEIR LIVES AND TIMES. IT MUST COMMUNICATE ... I CONSIDER MYSELF A MODERN ARTIST OR RATHER AN ARTIST OF TODAY ... BECAUSE I AM INFLUENCED BY THE THOUGHTS, THE LIFE AND THE AESTHETICS OF OUR TIME. I AM ALSO AN INHERIT OF MANY GREAT PAINTERS WHO PRECEEDED ME AND MADE TRADITION LIVING, ON-GOING AND EVER RENEWABLE LIKE NATUR ITSELF, BY FINDING DYNAMIC, CONTEMPORARY AND PERSONAL WAYS TO DEPICT AND INTERPRET *THEIR* LIFE AND *THEIR* TIME. "

—— *RAPHAEL SOYER*

16

STUDY OF JAY LYNCH AT THE BUSY BEE RESTAURANT — CHICAGO AUGUST 17, 1995

"YOU GET WHAT YOU DRAW!" — JAY LYNCH

(18)

LIVE AT
THE
VOLETS
VERTS!

STUDY of
NANCY
DORKING,
A
CALIFORNIA
GIRL IN
THE SOUTH
OF
FRANCE!

DECEMBER 30 1995

⑲

CATHERINE IN ANGOULÊME
- SALLE NEMO - CNDBI JAN 27, 1996

(20)

SUR LA TERRACE À LA
FÊTE MÉDIÉVALE
SAUVE ~ JUILLET 20th 1996.

ÊTRE
"TO BE"

JE SUIS
TU ES
IL/ELLE EST
NOUS SOMMES
VOUS ÊTES
ILS/ELLES SONT

21

" BEHIND
EVERY
GREAT
FORTUNE
LIES A
GREAT
CRIME. "

GUY IN
NÎMES

BRUNO AT LE COMMERCE

"THERE ARE TWO WAYS TO GET ENOUGH. ONE IS TO ACCUMULATE MORE AND MORE. THE OTHER IS TO DESIRE LESS."
— G. K. CHESTERTON

ST. CHRISTOL FLEA MARKET

24

RED HAIRED GIRL
IN LE MICOCOULIER
SEPTEMBER 1996

NIMES
NOV 13 1996

26

BUS
STATION.

WAITRESS AT
THE NÎMES
TRAIN
STATION

GUY READING ON
THE TGV TO PARIS.

STUDY OF
BOB,
THE COOK,
AT SMITTIE'S
NORTHAMPTON
DEC 27 1996

"I LIKED TO WATCH THE FIGHTS. SOMEHOW IT REMINDED ME
 WRITING. YOU NEED THE SAME THING, TALENT, GUTS AND
NDITION. ONLY THE CONDITION WAS MENTAL, SPIRITUAL. YOU
ERE NEVER A WRITER. YOU HAD TO *BECOME* A WRITER
CH TIME YOU SAT DOWN TO THE MACHINE. IT WASN'T
AT HARD ONCE YOU SAT DOWN IN FRONT OF THE MACHINE.
HAT WAS HARD SOMETIMES WAS FINDING THAT CHAIR AND
TTING IN IT. SOMETIMES YOU COULDN'T SIT IN IT. LIKE
ERYBODY ELSE IN THE WORLD, FOR YOU, THINGS GOT IN THE
AY: SMALL TROUBLES, BIG TROUBLES, CONTINUOUS SLAMMINGS
D BANGINGS. YOU HAD TO BE IN CONDITION TO ENDURE WHAT
AS TRYING TO KILL YOU. THAT'S THE MESSAGE I GOT FROM
ATCHING THE FIGHTS, OR WATCHING THE HORSES RUN, OR THE
AY THE JOCKS KEPT OVERCOMING BAD LUCK, SPILLS ON THE
RACK. I WROTE ABOUT LIFE, HA HA. BUT WHAT REALLY ASTON-
HED ME WAS THE IMMENSE COURAGE OF SOME OF THE PEOPLE
IVING THAT LIFE. THAT KEPT ME GOING."
—— CHARLES BUKOWSKI, "HOLLYWOOD" pgs 216 - 217. (29)

STUDY of A
GIRL At PANDA
GARDEN-CHRISTMAS
DAY 1996
NORTHAMPTON
MASSACHUSETTS

"PHOTOGRAPHY IS SUCH A RETARD
PROFESSION, AND THE PEOPLE IN IT ARE
SUCH PARASITES ON TECHNOLOGY. PHOTOGRA-
PHY HAS BECOME AN ALL-MONEY DEAL.
MONEY   KILLS CREATIVITY. ALL
THIS TECHNICAL EQUIPMENT, DOZENS
OF CREW - IT'S COMPLETE BULLSHIT.
IT DESTROYS THE MAGIC, "

— PETER BEARD
"WILD LIFE PHOTOGRAPHER"
AUTHOR OF "THE END OF THE GAME"
- VANITY FAIR NOV 96 Pg 216

(HAD
"DRAGON - PHOENIX"
DINNER)
(LOBSTER + CHICKEN)

30

MISS FLORENCE DINER
JANUARY 1, 1997

BREAKFAST

MY NEW
PORT OF CALL:
LA MAISON DU
JEAN-PIERRE
MERCIER À
SAUVE.
JUNE 1997

STAIRWAY TO MY STUDIO!

33

KARINE HERRYGERS
READING COMIC
BOOK IN PUBLIC
AND LAUGHING OUT
LOUD.
AUGUST 1997

STUDY OF
"ZAPATA"
AT
"LE COMMERCE"
SAUVE

RUE EGLISE NEUVE
SAUVE

36

37

38 CABIN IN THE
MER DES ROCHERS

STUDY OF
TONY
BALDWIN AT
THE CRUMB'S

MAXON

40

JAGUAR LEGS!

STUDY of
NICOLE SIVY
MAKING A SALAD

41

HEAD
STUDIES

CENTRE NATIONAL DE CRÉATION
DES ARTS DE LA RUE
ST. HENRI - MARSEILLE

42

STUDY OF DIMITRI SHIPOUNOFF 12·23·97

43

44

45

BEAUTIFUL NURSES!!
DANGEROUS WOMEN!!

STUDY OF LAURENCE RIEUTORD

46

STUDY OF
FABIENNE
CERDAN

47

LUNCH CROWD AT THE
BUFFET GARE
NÎMES
(I'M ON MY WAY TO
ANGOULÊME)
JANUARY 22, 1998

STUDY AT
'LE TERMINUS' BAR
NÎMES... 2/11/98

(50)

LA PETITE BOURSE NÎMES

LA PETITE BOURSE
NIMES 2·11·98

53

55

PARIS ...3 MINUTE HEADS

METRO

AT THE LOUVRE...

56

"I'M JUST LOOKING FOR PATTERNS IN THE CHAOS..." QUOTE FROM "Contact"

TIM VAN BEEK AT PERRY'S CHERRY DINER - 03-07-98 ... STURGEON BAY, WISCONSIN

58

JEANETTE JACQMIN AT BAY FAMILY EAST... MAY 13 '98

3 MINUTE HEADS

"MEETAY OIDPA, OITUMURA AKE-ETAY."

(a definition of life written in Maa, the
Maasai language. It means living passionately
for today and purposefully for tomorrow. You can
only enjoy NOW. Being happy TODAY is the real
proof of success.) Repacking Your Bags py 220

3 minute heads

"THE MIND IS ITS OWN PLACE, AND THE PLACES INHABITED BY THE INSANE AND THE EXCEPTIONALLY GIFTED ARE SO DIFFERENT FROM THE PLACES WHERE ORDINARY MEN AND WOMEN LIVE, THAT THERE IS LITTLE OR NO COMMON GROUND OF MEMORY TO SERVE AS A BASIS FOR UNDERSTANDING OR FELLOW FEELING. WORDS ARE UTTERED, BUT FAIL TO ENLIGHTEN."
———— ALDOUS HUXLEY

ZORRO AUTOPORTRAIT !! MAY 1998

"THE QUALITY OF OUR UNDERSTANDING DEPENDS DECISIVELY ON THE DETACHMENT, OBJECTIVITY, AND CARE WITH WHICH WE LEARN TO STUDY OURSELVES — BOTH WHAT GOES ON INSIDE US AND HOW WE APPEAR AS OBJECTIVE PHENOMENA IN THE EYES OF OTHERS."
—— E. F. SCHUMACHER
(A GUIDE FOR THE PERPLEXED) 1977

AN OLD VICTOR MUG

"WE ARE WHAT WE PRETEND TO BE, SO WE MUST BE CAREFUL ABOUT WHAT WE PRETEND TO BE,"
—— KURT VONNEGUT, JR.

3 minute heads

"ONE'S FIRST TASK IS TO LEARN FROM SOCIETY AND "TRADITION" AND TO FIND ONES'S TEMPORARY HAPPINESS IN RECEIVING DIRECTIONS FROM OUTSIDE."

CONTINUE ⟶

64

3 MINUTE HEADS...

⊕ "ONE'S SECOND TASK IS TO INTERIORIZE THE KNOW-
LEDGE ONE HAS GAINED, TO SORT OUT, KEEPING THE
GOOD AND JETTISONING THE BAD ; THIS IS THE PROCESS
OF BECOMING SELF-DIRECTED."

CONTINUE ⟶

3 MINUTE HEADS

"ONE'S THIRD TASK IS TO ABANDON ONE'S LIKES AND DISLIKES, ALL OF ONE'S EGOCENTRIC PREOCCUPATIONS. TO THE EXTENT THAT ONE SUCCEEDS IN THIS, ONE CEASES TO BE DIRECTED FROM OUTSIDE, AND ALSO CEASES TO BE SELF-DIRECTED. ONE HAS GAINED FREEDOM OR, ONE MIGHT SAY, ONE IS THEN GOD-DIRECTED."
—E. F. SCHUMACHER

3 MINUTE HEADS...

"SINCE PEOPLE DON'T KNOW WHETHER THEY WILL LIKE A MOVIE UNTIL THEY SEE IT, THEY HAVE TO RELY ON WHAT OTHERS TELL THEM. IF THEY HEAR GOOD THINGS — FROM FRIENDS, CRITICS, OR WHOMEVER —— THEY WILL PROBABLY GO AND SEE THE FILM; IF THEY HEAR BAD THINGS, THEY WON'T. ECONOMISTS CALL THIS PROCESS AN **INFORMATION CASCADE**..."
—— JOHN CASSIDY - THE NEW YORKER

3 MINUTE HEADS...

" NORMAL HUMAN THOUGHT AND PERCEPTION IS MARKED NOT BY ACCURACY BUT BY POSITIVE SELF-ENHANCING ILLUSIONS ABOUT THE SELF, THE WORLD, AND THE FUTURE. "

— — SHELLY TAYLOR *POSITIVE ILLUSIONS*.

3 Minute.....heads....

"WHAT ONE BELIEVES TO BE TRUE EITHER IS TRUE OR BECOMES TRUE IN ONE'S MIND, WITHIN LIMITS TO BE DETERMINED EXPERIMENTALLY AND EXPERIENTIALLY. THESE LIMITS ARE BELIEFS TO BE TRANSCENDED." — JOHN LILLY *THE CENTRE OF THE CYCLONE*

OUTLINES ON THE METRO

PLEASE GOD... SEND ME A CUTE FRENCH GIRL!

MASS AT NOTRE DAME · PARIS 12·07·98

71

Labori

GARDON du
MIALET.
(near St Jean
du GARD...
5 km.)

AT THE RIVER...

14 Juillet 1998.

73

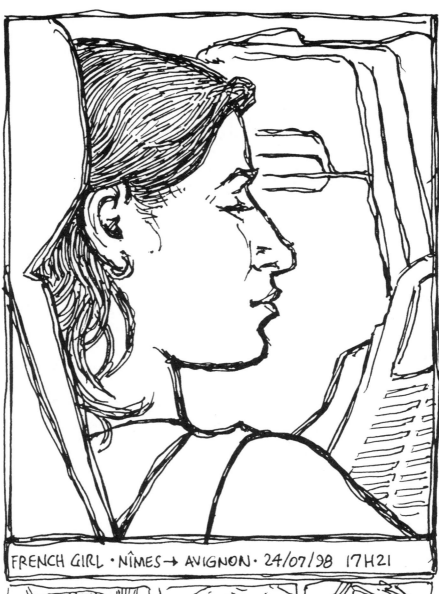

FRENCH GIRL · NÎMES → AVIGNON · 24/07/98 17H21

Catherine KREMER · Jean·Claude LEPORTIER · Alain SCHONS

les pilozofes

La Mémé

GRODO

PENARD

PUPPET SHOW AT THEATRE DU BOURG-NEUF
AVIGNON "LES PHILOSOPHES"
24·07·98

(75)

BERNARDO

DOÑA ISAURA & DON DI

HERVÉ CRISTIANINI AS
BERNARDO

AVEC
CHRISTINE
  GAYA AS
   DOÑA ISAURA
CAROLINE RUIZ
   AS DOÑA LUNA
LAURE DESSERTINE
   AS SGT SANCHEZ
ALI BOUGUERABA
ALI MEHIGUENI
BERNADETTE
  BALALAS

MISE EN SCÈNE ET SCÉNARIO:
     FRED MUHL
DIALOGUES:
  JEAN-MARC MICHELANGELI
CHORÉGRAPHIE:
     INÈS NUNCA

JULIEN
ASSELIN AS
COLONEL
MIGUEL
SANTOS Y
BURNOS

76

LESS THAN 3 minute heads

ON THE RUE DES TEINTURIERS IN AVIGNON...

(they seem to be "REASONABLE LIKENESSES.")

"IT IS IN SELF-LIMITATION THAT A MASTER FIRST SHOWS HIMSELF." — GOETHE

WOMEN READING
AT THE BRASSERIE LA RÉGENCE

SAMEDI · 25-07-98 · AVIGNON

Petit EVA

82

DAVID ARAZIE IN FRANCE...

AUGUST 23, 1998 · LE MICOCOULIER · SAUVE

"60 THOUSAND DOLLARS? THAT'S NOTHIN'!
60 THOUSAND DOLLARS IS NOTHIN'!"
—— DAVID ARAZIE

83

3 MINUTE HEADS in SAUVE.

"PARODIES AND CARICATURES ARE THE MOST PENETRATING OF CRITICISMS." — ALDOUS HUXLEY

"LIFE IS THE PROCESS BY MEANS OF WHICH DEATH
CHALLENGES US. DEATH IS THE ACTIVE FORCE. LIFE
IS THE ARENA. AND IN THAT ARENA THERE ARE ONLY
TWO CONTENDERS AT ANY TIME: ONESELF AND DEATH."
—— CARLOS CASTANEDA
" THE POWER OF SILENCE"

86

FINISHED/UNFINISHED...
STUDIES DONE IN THE ACCADEMIA IN FIRENZE
(MY FOURTEENTH VISIT TO ITALY) - SEPTEMBRE 11 1998

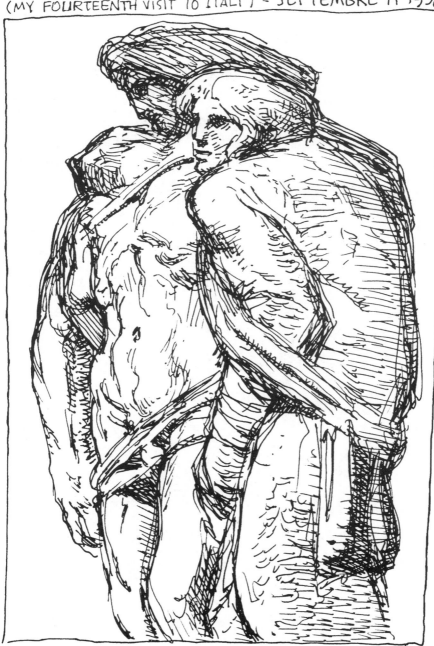

TESTE di TRE MINUTI

DISTAT ENIM QUAE / SYDERA TE EXCIPIANT

"THE DESTINY OF MANKIND DEPENDS ON THE LUCKY OR UNLUCKY STARS UNDER WHICH EACH PERSON IS BORN." —VI SATIRE OF GIOVENALE — CAMERA DEI VENTI (O DELLO ZODIACO) PALAZZO TE

Teste di Tre Minuti

"FABRUM ESSE SWAE QUEMQUE FORTUNAE"
"EACH MAN THE ARCHITECT OF HIS OWN
FATE." — Appius Caecus 4th cent BC

89

TESTE DI TRE MINUTI

" THE UNIVERSE IS TRANSFORMATION; OUR
LIFE IS WHAT OUR THOUGHTS MAKE IT. "
———— Marcus Aurelius 121-180 AD.

TesTe di Tre minuTi a ROMA...

" GENIUS IS FORMED IN QUIET, CHARACTER
IN THE STREAM OF HUMAN LIFE."
—— GOETHE

"ARTISTS ARE UNCONTROLLABLE!"
——FRANK STACK (CONSPIRACY·THEORIST) IN SAUVE.

NICOLE IN NÎMES...

GREGG the GREEK.

SARAH BRYANT at LE COMMERCE · SAUVE

27 OCTOBRE 1998

95

Millie Dolan

AT LA TOUR DE MOLE --- NOVEMBER 13TH, 1998..

3-MINUTE HEADS

" THE REASONS OF THE HEART IS NOT THE
HEART OF REASON. "
———— OLD FRENCH SAYING.
(PASCAL)

ON THE METRO...

RED SHOE
LERK IN
PARIS

99

ON LE MÉTRO.

1999

101

PARIS ··· IN THE LOUVRE ···

"PERSONNAGE EN COSTUME CIVIL ET COIFFÉ D'UN BONNET À JUGBLAIRE, REPRÉSENTÉ ASSIS, SUPPORTANT LA BASE D'UNE COLONNE.

ITALIE DU NORD, XIIIᵉ SIÈCLE

COULD THIS BE THE INSPIRATION FOR VICTOR HUGO TO CREATE THE CHARACTER OF QUASIMODO?

29 - JANUARY - 1999

102

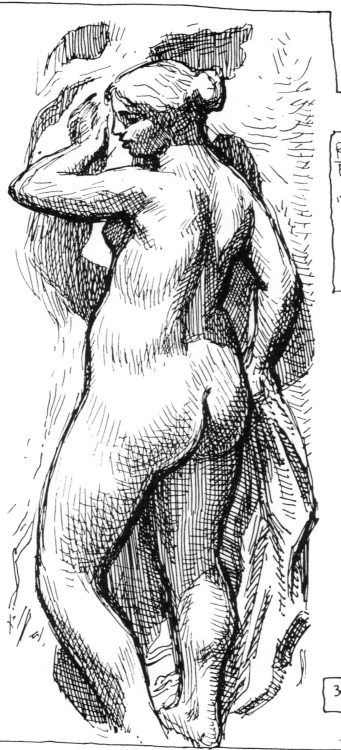

RENOIR
FIGURE
FROM
" LE
JUGEMENT
DE PÂRIS".
1914
PLÂTRE

30 · JANUARY
- 1999

103

(DANS)
SUR LE MÉTRO...

"THE EXERCISE OF DISCIPLINE"

104

MEETING AT RESTAURANT MA BOURGOGNE - PLACE DES VOSGES - PARIS

105

SOMEWHERE IN SAUVE.

"MY CAST OF MIND"

"ZERO PRIVACY"

111

CHANGE FOCUS" ⑬

ABITS OF PERCEPTION!"

117

TRICI VENOLA IN ROBERT CRUMB'S STUDIO ... SAUVE ... APRIL 17TH, 1999

118

PATTERNS of EXPERIENCE..."

119

"CLARITY OF PURPOSE"

A VIEW FROM THE TRAIN TO MADRID: A SPANISH TOWER.

" EVERY START UPON AN UNTRODDEN PATH IS A VENTURE WHICH ONLY IN
UNUSUAL CIRCUMSTANCES LOOKS SENSIBLE AND LIKELY TO SUCCE
—ALBERT SCHWEITZER

"AN ARTIST'S ONLY REAL COMPENSATION FOR HIS WORK IS IN THE DOING OF IT." — N. C. WYETH

127

RESTAURANT

"THE WISE MAN TRAVELS TO DISCOVER HIMSELF." —JAMES RUSSELL LOWELL

(129)

"THE RISKS OF INTIMACY..."

THE ILLUSION OF EMPOWERMENT..."

131

"PERSONAL MYTHOLOGY"

A CONSPIRACY BETWEEN DESIGN AND CHANCE."

"THE MOST IMPORTANT ISSUE IS THE FULLEST USE OF POTEN

NDIVIDUALITY IS IMPORTANT..."

HANNELORE ODER FERDINARD IN THE STUDIO...

136

...NNELORE EDER FERDINAND AND HER BACK...

" I FANCY THAT THE FACES THAT LOOK OUT AT
    US FROM THE DISTANT PAST ARE THE
    SUREST MEANING OF AN EPOCH. "

— KENNETH CLARK, *CIVILISATION*
    a PERSONAL VIEW, 1968.

AN ARCH IN QUISSAC ⟶ AUGUST 3, 1999

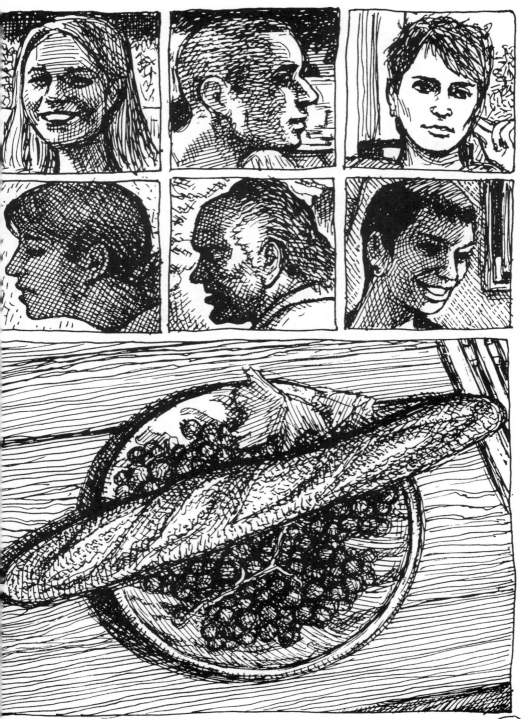

ONE NIGHT... AT THE *LE MICOCOULIER* RESTAURANT...

142 MAGGIE'S DAUGHTER DISCOURSES BETWEEN COURSES...

"HE REAL GOAL IS TU URN THE FACTORY AND HE DOGS WILL BE FREE!"

" THE MEDIA MILITATES AGAINST INNOCENCE, AND THOUGH YOU MIGHT BE TO FIND TRACES OF INNOCENCE IN REMOTE PARTS OF THE WORLD, IT'S DLY VANISHING AS THE STANDARDIZATION OF THOUGHT MES MORE AND MORE PERVASIVE. " —— WILLIAM BURROUGHS

14·3

STEPHANIE & GENOA

144

LANDSCAPE OF NOUNS "

145

147

FILIPPO
GAMBETTA

NA A LA MADDALENA BAR - GENOA

2000 AD

EPHRAIM, WISCONSIN - APRIL 9, 2000 153

"FOR THIS TIME."

YVES

TANIA

157

NANOU at LA TOUR DEMOLE

159

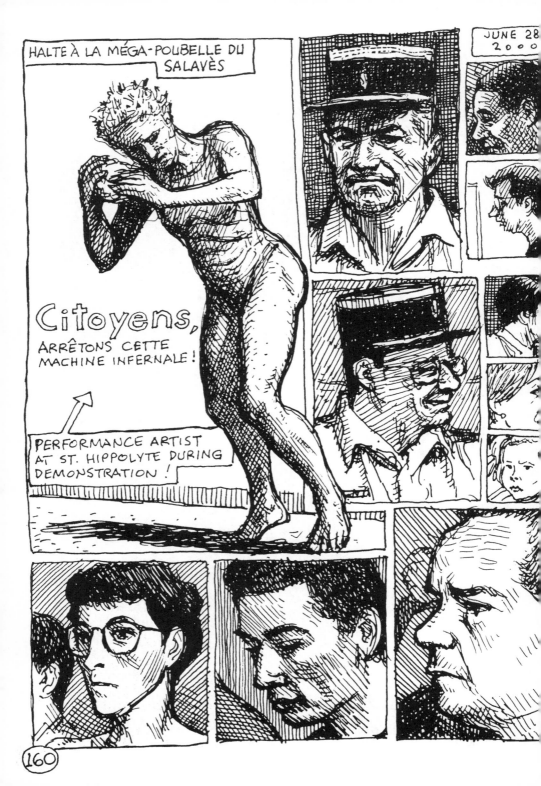

HALTE À LA MÉGA-POUBELLE DU SALAVÈS

JUNE 28 2000

Citoyens,
ARRÊTONS CETTE MACHINE INFERNALE!

PERFORMANCE ARTIST AT ST. HIPPOLYTE DURING DEMONSTRATION!

"LET'S DO IT AGAIN IN "F"..."

"ACTIVE STRUGGLE!!

162

GUERRIER COMBATTANT
DIT "GLADIATEUR
BORGHÈSE"
SIGNÉ PAR AGASIAS D'ÉPHÈSE,
FILS DE DOSITHÉOS   VERS 100 AV. JC
ANZIO (ANTIUM), PROVINCE DE LATIUM.

LOUVRE

164

165

"BE TRANSFORMED BY THE RENEWING OF YOUR MIND!"

167

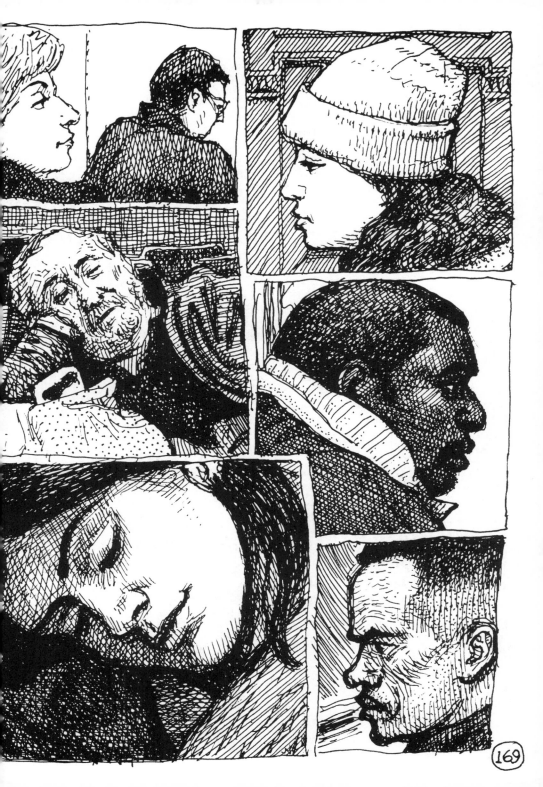

169

A COUR DES CHOSES' - THÉÂTRE d'O

171

173

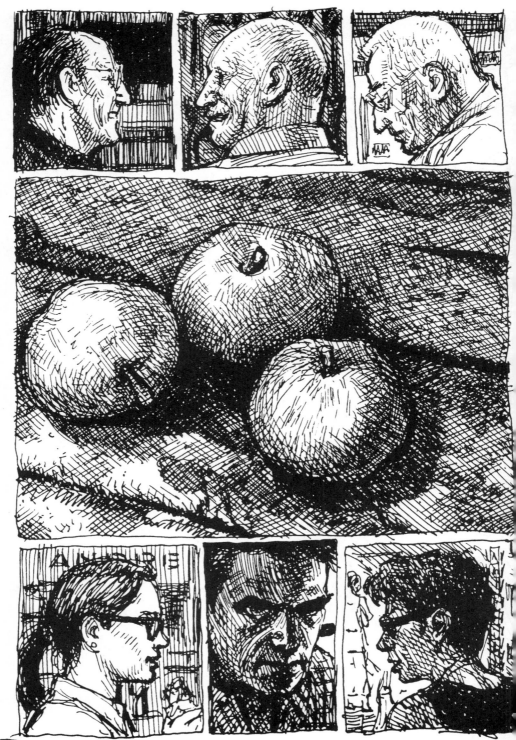

"CRISIS OF MEANING"

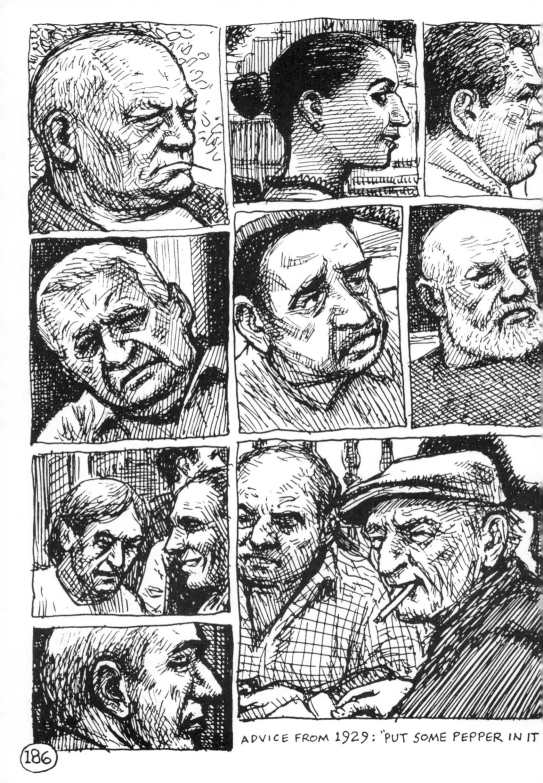

ADVICE FROM 1929: "PUT SOME PEPPER IN IT

188

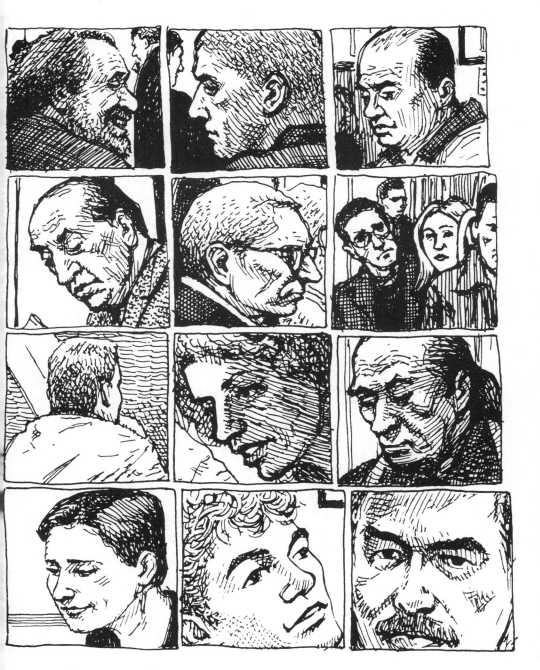

" TALENT DOES WHATEVER IT WANTS TO DO;
GENIUS ONLY WHAT IT CAN DO. "
——— EUGENE DELACROIX

189

"THINGS OF QUALITY HAVE
NO FEAR OF TIME."

RAC WINS! 82%

"A WORK OF ART IS NEVER FINISHED,
ONLY ABANDONED." — ANATOLE FRANCE

Rue
du Four

BOULANGERIE

202

the **WINE of KINGS and the KING of WINES.**

The CASTELLAS à SAUVÉ à UNE HEURE

AUGUST 16 200

RELIEF MITHRIAQUE À DOUBLE FACE · ROME
IIe - IIIe S. ap. J.C. - MARBRE SALLE 25

LA DIVINITÉ IRANIENNE MITHRA EST INTRODUITE À ROME DURANT LA
SECONDE MOITIÉ DU 1er S. après J.-C., SOUS la FORME D'UN CULT À
MYSTÈRES JALONNÉ DE RITES D'INITIATION. LE DIEU EST REPRÉ-
SENTÉ SUR UNE FACE DU RELIEF ÉGORGEANT LE TAUREAU POUR
FÉCONDER L'UNIVERS.; SUR L'AUTRE, IL BANQUETE AVEC LE SOLEIL,
AUQUEL IL EST ALORS ASSIMILÉ POUR SIGNIFIER LE TRIOMPHÉ
DE LA LUMIÈRE APRÈS LA VICTOIRE SUR LES FORCES NÉFASTES.

203

PERSONAL HISTORY

I began keeping sketchbooks in 1968 when I was in high school in Green Bay, Wisconsin, where my family lived. The small city was famous for its Green Bay Packers professional football team, while the state as a whole was known for beer, cheese, and recreational sports like hunting and fishing. At that time, northeastern Wisconsin qualified as "culturally deprived" and a federally funded program called Operation Area Arts (OAA) was set up to give high-school kids college level art instruction along with free supplies and studio space. Through this program, I studied oil painting and etching. It was there that I learned that drawing is the visual foundation of all the visual arts, and that keeping sketchbooks is something anyone seriously aspiring to be an artist should do.

I had already developed some pretty good figurative-drawing skills by copying from comic books, and for several years I assisted a slightly older artist and friend of mine, Dale Kuipers, on his ambitious 8mm stop-action animation film, *Infant Earth*. We created concept sketches, storyboard drawings, and background paintings as well as tabletop sets, handcrafted poseable foam-rubber dinosaurs, and other three-dimensional props. We were self-taught students of the mass media, raised on comic books, television, and movies. Art in museums would come later.

I like to refer to all this media input as "art triggers" (see pages 204-205), and the fallout from all this cultural radioactivity caused infinite mutations. As a small child I copied animated cartoon characters, but it was probably my pride of ownership of a 1956 *Superman* "S" belt from Kellogg's Corn Flakes that amused my Aunt Lorraine, causing her to buy me my first *Superman* comic book. I couldn't read it, but I copied the Superman flying poses (drawn by Wayne Boring) over and over. Then followed the Dell *Zorro* comics drawn by Alex Toth, whose drawings of fencing poses and fold concepts in Zorro's cape challenged me. By the time I was eight years old, the habit of collecting, reading, and drawing from comics was well established.

My favorite cartoonists were Dick Sprang *(Batman)*, George Papp *(Superboy)*, Carmine Infantino *(The Flash)*, Gil Kane *(Green Lantern* and *The Atom)*,

Mike Sekowski *(Justice League)*, Joe Kubert *(Hawkman)*, Jesse Marsh *(Tarzan)*, Steve Ditko *(Spider-Man)*, Jack Kirby *(Fantastic Four)*, Sy Barry *(The Phantom)*, Boring, Toth, and others. For me, these comic books were sort of a correspondence school of figure drawing. I still learn when I reread them. The cartoonists who drew them were great teachers.

Left alone, I might have become a full-time cartoonist or professional illustrator—actually, I worked freelance for Kitchen Sink Press for thirty years, never making a single deadline!—but my etching teacher at OAA, Richard J. Olsen, imparted "heavy stuff" to me about being an artist. This was often accompanied by raucous laughter and a stinging slap between the shoulder blades. I was sixteen then, and brought examples of my then-current art heroes to show Olé: Hal Foster *(Prince Valiant)*, Frank Frazetta *(Conan the Conqueror)* and Neal Adams *(Deadman)*. He threw his head back, laughed, and told me, "It's time you looked at the *good* stuff, Ace!" He pulled out books on Goya's *The Disasters of War* and the *Los Caprichos* etchings for me to study.

Later, during my first visit to the Art Institute of Chicago, Olé stood me before Henri Toulouse-Lautrec's *At the Moulin Rouge,* pointing out Lautrec's self-portrait in the midst of a large crowd of dancers, drunks, and friends. In it, the artist himself, with his guardian, tours the legendary Parisian dance hall, almost like Dante escorted by the shade of Virgil in the *Inferno.*

"Look at all the faces of this crowd, Ace," Olé chuckled. "Some of them are really out of it! See the blue face of this dancer in the lower right corner? That's because Lautrec wanted to capture the effect of artificial lighting on her. This is how the artist looks at the world. He has to see everything and then remake the experience of what he saw from the artist's point of view. Everyone sees things differently. The artist looks 'hard' and feels it in his 'guts.' Great art always has 'guts!'"

Then, with a sweep of his arm which seemed to make the crowd at the Art Institute an extension of the crowd in Lautrec's picture, Olé said, "The artist is always out there, looking and working, forging the steel!" Olé often referred to the making of art as "forging the steel." No matter what the medium, a work of art was the result of decision making and problem solving, and when you looked hard there would be evidence of a personal battle fought as the artist attempted to translate an idea or an experience into a concrete material form.

Magically, this early experience gave me direction, and later I vowed to see every great masterpiece of art in the original, a task which I am near to completing thirty-four years later. Richard J. Olsen told me then what he probably tells his students at the University of Georgia-Athens today, and it's what all the great masters of art have always said: look at nature, draw from life, study your fellow man, and then create something that sums up what it means to be human. Artists slow the world down so that other people can share and experience reality in a different way through a different pair of eyes.

While all this sounds serious, the real attitude to have is that it's all really just a game. Before I discovered the great masters of art, my role models, as noted, were the adventure heroes of comic books, TV, and movies. My cultural programming was to follow the example of Zorro, Superman, and The Lone Ranger for truth and justice. For me, to be an artist in today's world is a heroic act of will, and a search for truth and meaning that makes life a great adventure. Drawing in sketchbooks is fun, but it is also a very important discipline to develop. Over time, these sketches add up and can be consulted, showing how an artist thinks and grows, who he was, and where he might be going. I begin almost each day with a *grand cremè* (French coffee with milk) at a street cafe and the question, "Who are these people I am sharing this moment with?" I open my sketchbook and make some lines on a page. This book is a collection of just some of those many pages—lines made over the past ten years, mostly in Europe on the way to visit one museum or another.

It all starts looking like a comic strip, doesn't it? Funny. Art has a life of its own.

—Peter Poplaski
Au Rond Point, Paris
August 19, 2002